ask your undertaker

ask your undertaker

ADAM MATCHO

WPA Press
Pittsburgh, Pennsylvania

Book Layout & Design: Michelle Boring
Cover Art : Phelan Newman

TABLE OF CONTENTS

For Mike and Fran

One Week Notice

The boss told me, "We're sorry
to lose a worker like you. But
we'll both forge new paths forward."

The boss told me, "I really wish
you'd given me more time
to find your replacement. I mean,
you've only given me one week."

"And eight years," I corrected.

PART ONE

Petra, From Work

Management called her over the loudspeaker, "Petra,
please come to the hardware department. Immediately."

It was her husband, John, no shoes, jeans half down,
disoriented. A dead vegetable scent all over the store.

He knocked over the garbage can display and Petra
asked me if she should leave and drive him home.

"He can't do this here, where I work," she said, her broken
accent from a land near Russia or Romania, somewhere

far from Pennsylvania, where we work in a grocery store.
A manager told her, "Clock out and please take care of that."

That was John, who had two heart attacks and had been in bad
health ever since. Petra said he'd been on so many pills ever since.

Petra's thin hands shook at the time clock, so I slid her card
for her and she said, "I don't know if I'll be here tomorrow."

I still breathed the musty odor John left
when my shift ended a half hour later.

Unexpected traffic had me cursing cars,
weaving to see what had us backed up.

A broke down rusted out pickup pulled
to the shoulder had us down to one lane.

I passed and saw Petra, from work, pacing and petting
a small brown terrier. John's jeans were around his knees,

his hands clutched the guardrail while he hunched
over the side, talking shit to the ground. I parked.

My friend, Lori, told me: kindness is when you help
someone who can do absolutely nothing for you.

Lori says wise things like that. She knows
about pain because she knows about kindness.

I didn't want to stop. My shift was 10 hours
long and my family had dinner on the table.

"Our truck," Petra cried. "It just stopped. We have
dinner in the back and John does this business now."

John's business was spitting into the gravel
and shouting, "Show it to me!" to nobody,

or maybe somebody. Maybe he was wailing
at the world in general, all the way to hell.

I wanted to help but didn't know how.
I could smell John, stronger than before.

It was a scent like the dirt that worked
itself under your nails and stuck there.

"Here's what I can do," I said. "Petra, give me
the dog. You check what's going on with John."

She dropped the terrier into my arms
and he shivered until he snuggled.

I said, "What's his name?"
Petra said, "Brutus."

I said, "It's okay, Brutus."
The dog had the smell all over

my clothes, as I soothed Brutus
and brushed the ash smashed into his fur.

6

Petra pulled her husband's pants up, tightened
his belt and attempted to get him to the truck.

"We can go sit in there," she said. "There's nothing
for you to see out here in the dirt. It's all in the truck."

"Petra!" I said. "Is it okay, if I call the cops?"
I always ask others before I call the police.

I told 911 it was a medical emergency.
I said, "Maybe not. I'm not a doctor."

I said, "I work at a grocery store with her
and now they are stranded and need help."

Petra stammered over, arms rigid and crossed
until she reached us and talked to Brutus.

She said, "It will be okay, puppy. You have
a friend here. He's one of the good ones."

When the cop parked behind the dead truck, I handed
Brutus over, but wanted to give him a warm bubble bath.

I told the officer what I knew, which wasn't
much and she asked if they were on drugs.

I said, "Drugs?"
I said, "I don't think so."

I spoke like I was under oath, hand on an invisible
bible. I wanted to say something helpful and true.

I said, "I'm not a doctor. Just some
guy who works at a grocery store."

The cop told me to go,
so I crossed the highway,

between the traffic that blurred by, kicking
up a draft hard enough to knock me down.

Helping My Mother Call Off Work

She is worried about screwing someone over.
"It's a Saturday," she says. "Nobody
wants to be called in on a Saturday."

I tell her she'll be fine. She requested this day off
months ago. Rejected once, since it was the weekend.
But she resubmitted. She explained to management.

Her only daughter. My sister. The last
of her four children is graduating
with the highest honors of them all.

She's worried she won't sound sick enough
on the phone. "How's this?" she says, soft
and weak, my mother from her deathbed.

She's had this job 13 years and called off exactly twice.
Once for the funeral of her favorite aunt, and once when
she went to the ER the night before with stomach pains.

I remember the other side of this stalwart reliability:
the after-school chore lists, dinner notes on the oven,
me, the oldest, in charge of my brothers and sister.

My sister, who is graduating Saturday, and
my mom paralyzed with the idea of using
her accumulated 136 PTO hours to attend.

I say, "It's not like they're doing you
a favor. You've earned this time off.
It's part of your benefit package."

She says, "Your sister is killing me, you know."
She says, "I just hope my boss isn't mad." She says,
"Okay, give me that phone" and made the call.

9

My Grandmother, The Seamstress

Sundays were her day off
from the bedding factory
on Eisenhower Boulevard
where my she stitched
mattresses and sewed pillows
put us all to sleep
swaddled tight with the work
of her hummingbird hands.

But Sundays she left church
after Communion
to roll raw meatballs
with quick hands,
efficient and tireless.

Cooked pasta strung its scent
through the air by the time
our dress shoes were slipped
off and we ambled in black socks
the family slotted in the usual seats
and my grandmother, her day off,
wiped red sauce from the sleeve
her poufy blue church blouse.

My Grandfather, the Borough Worker

The first one awake, he'd set
the electric heater, steam
coffee and lay out

the newspaper
at my seat so I could read
to him over breakfast.

Local news. Weather
disasters. Human disasters.
Sports. The Funnies.

Whatever he picked
I read and he helped
with words I didn't know.

My grandfather never finished
grade school. He closed his large hands
into fists and punched a timeclock.

"It was tough," he said. "They didn't
want to hire Italians. You had to
show them what you were capable."

He got on with the borough. Plowed snow.
Filled potholes and paved roads. He unflooded
basements where the water wrinkled his hands.

The Spider

Death peeks through a crack
in your bedroom curtains, owl-eyed,
slips beneath the cellar door, into the basement,
sets up a spider web in an unlit corner,

so when you step through its silk tripwire
and swat the single strand of silk stuck
to your face and the full infinity
of the web comes into view, you freeze

with the thought of the spider,
its kaleidoscope sight on you,
all those eyes wondering
what exactly it caught today.

Race Relations, Northmoreland Park, circa 2015

Our dog is brown and black
and trots beside us at the lake.
We walk around most evenings
and today a girl, a black
teenaged girl, runs up the grass
bank, away from hissing geese
and people with leashed dogs.

We are mostly white people
out here in suburban country
and notice teenaged black girls
even when we try to not admit
we notice teenaged black girls.

Headphones and track shoes
this girl trudges up the hill
knees high, arms churning
then half-jogs to the bottom
and takes time to breathe.

Second time around
my wife, the dog and me
we see her ready to blaze
a runner on the blocks
and the dog barks
at a passing pickup
some young white kid
yelling from the cab
and we only hear half:
"—GGER"
and we stop dead, exchange
a look to make sure
we heard what we heard.

13

My wife and I
and hopefully
our dog
are furious
and embarrassed
and privileged
and used to this
and we stop
with how we feel
and look to the teen
who this hateful syllable
was directed, and she's got
her headphones on, eyes
fixed ahead as she climbs
her hill yet again.

Daily Death of a Parent

My four-year-old wants fruit snacks
instead of dinner. I tell him take two
more bites of chicken.

"See how this works,"
I say, hoping I'm a wise
and friendly owl to him.

He tastes a thin, skinless slice
and before I can turn my head
around he spits it into his hand,

smashes his half-chewed chicken
into the wall and looks at me to see
if I understand how this really works.

Gross

It costs $20 for my kid
to eat school lunch every day,
unless our two-parent family
earns less than $1500 each pay.

I ferret through paystubs,
shake them like lottery tickets
at my wife, show her
we don't bring home $1500.

This is a break, I think, but
she is depressed from work
every day. Working more
than being home with

a busted hot water heater
a rattling refrigerator
a sick cat, a son we struggle
to feed without assistance.

Then she says, "They judge
by your gross income, not
what we actually keep."

And I see we make
$1600, the two of us
every two weeks. Gross.

Which sounds like money, but
there are taxes and health care,
Social Security and 401k plans
I'm sure are being siphoned away

by some hedge fund fuckface
who doesn't stress about money

for his dog's vet bill and certainly
not his son eating lunch each day.

After that, we fall below
every benchmark and still spread
our money further for shelter and
electricity and copays and no matter

what, my kid needs to eat
lunch, every day,
and that costs $20 a week.
Gross.

The Luxury of Dreams

You say you wake so quickly, you
don't remember your dreams.

Most days start ten minutes late
then a meeting morning, where

all the old hacks talk and talk and talk and
it's all weather and television and more work,

same pay. The same ones who need told never hear
a word, and there's you, 10 years now in one place

can't call a day off without taking shit
from incompetent middle management.

The way we have to work, make our money
just to give it all away, so work becomes life

and that's what we're talking about here.
At home, we call coworkers by their names

and we know them from other stories,
other atrocities. You say they fishtank us.

Stack us in cubicles like the ash of the dead
sealed in stone mausoleums. And when it's time,

when the company has to choose between you
and fiscal projections, it's no decision.

You're gone. Besides, they already sucked
your soul through a straw some time ago.

In spite of this truth,
you're burning up the backroad

just to punch in before the clock
rounds up, steals your time.

Through the flus and heartbreak, depressed
mornings stuck under the covers.

Even your sleep is work.
No rest. No dreams.

And tomorrow's Wednesday.
And now tomorrow's here

and there you go, sleep still stuck
in your eye, because you have to.

And even though I think you deserve
something more than a poem

about that kind of grit, these are
lean times, baby, and until somebody

figures a way to get poets paid, this
is as good as it gets for people like us.

A Serious Question

Here's a teen, muscled under
his Gateway Gators wrestling
shirt, pocked with youthful acne
belting his best James Brown—
I feel good—into a boxed
hot pink mini massager.

His girlfriend, thin as laces
on dress shoes, giggles and dances
something like The Swim
in the middle of the walkway.

Startled, when I ask how I can
help, the teen cut his retail karaoke
and ponders the now-smashed box
and says, "How much for this dildo?"
and they laugh. It was that funny.

Working
at the kind of store I do, you get
some odd questions. You get
all the mallrats. Mostly you get
run down, ready for the days
to be nights as soon as you wake.

"It's not a dildo, it's a vibrator,"
I corrected.

The teen and his girl
stop laughing.

He says, "Oh yeah?
What's the difference?"

"One vibrates. One doesn't," I say.
"Which one are you?"

It's 2:37 a.m. In Conemaugh Valley Memorial Hospital Emergency Room

for Adrienne

And this guy refuses to sit in the waiting area. Facedown
on a paper sheet on a small bed he tells the nurse his story.

This nurse, she's only halfway through her all-nighter.
She knows there is a glass cigar case lodged in his rectum.

He holds his hand in the air, swears. He was cleaning his jeep
naked and fell back onto the glass case, which was positioned

in such a way that it bulleted up into his ass. The nurse stops
jotting her notes and says, "So, that's what you're going with?"

Race Relations, Pittsburgh Mills Mall, circa 2007

We sold onesies. Twenty dollar
baby rompers with sayings
like They Shake Me, and It's
Lunchtime: Where's The Titties?

This mall was a dying mall
so when the family of four
began to browse, they were
the only ones in the store.

The teenage son took a onesie
behind the tee shirt cube and
reappeared emptyhanded like
some shoplifting magic trick.

The truth behind the illusion was stuffed
into the cubby of the tee shirt cube:
a broken hanger, a ripped price tag.
I said, "You want to pay for that?"

His mom and his sisters were there
in seconds but he clutched his bag
from some other store, the bag
I'm sure he stashed the onesie.

His mother grabbed the little sister's
hand and said, "Christopher?" and
Christopher said, "I didn't do shit."
and his older sister pointed at my face.

She said, "Would you accuse a white family
of this?" and I nodded, said, "If they stole it?
Absolutely." A sadness blanketed the mother
and she looked to her son, "Christopher?"

Christopher unrolled a denim pant leg
from his shopping bag like a scarf from
a clown's throat, but I said, "Dump it
on the counter if you expect me to believe that."

Christopher stepped closer, said,
"What time do you get out of here,
bitch?" and I laughed and asked,
"You want to fight because you got caught

stealing baby clothes?" Christopher
looked at his mom and said, "I'm
about to fuck this white boy up."
I pointed the portable phone's antenna

at him like a sniper laser.
I said, "I'll have the cops
here in a minute," but his
sister snapped open her purse.

I poked my finger
at Christopher, "See?
You know you're wrong
and she's paying for it."

"How much is it?" the sister said
at the register, ready to go. I told
her twenty and she said, "For
a baby shirt? That's a ripoff."

I shrugged, said, "He's didn't
have to steal it." She tossed a bill
at me, said, "Whatever. I run
my own business. I probably make

more in a day than you do
all year. So enjoy your
dead end job." And even though
I wanted to snap back, maybe

tell her to go fuck herself
I didn't. The truth was I
had bills and debts and
badly needed the work.

Sometimes

Sometimes, since my job
requires little creativity
and my days taper,
predictable as a bad cop
drama, and if I wake once
before my 5 a.m. alarm
I wake with the dog and
the work stress creeps in
and I'm restless and cracked
up before I even clock in.

I question if grad school
could save me, if grad school,
an MFA, another $30,000 wave
of loans I'm already swimming in
would make me a better poet, or
possibly a worse poet but more
ambitious about it, maybe
a pretentious careerist poet who
writes for other pretentious
careerist poets who teach
each other's books and cram the
literary canon like a garbage disposal.

Sometimes
I don't think
about school.

I'm dead from freight throwing,
shelf stocking, cardboard boxes
that dry you out and crack
your skin open and send you
home with bloody fingers,
dirt under the nails, dead
from living and breathing

the black mold growing
in our basement with my
family, each member another
job—trips to the orthodontist,
showing up to support
the marching band before
they cut funding again, ICU
visits to my grandmother
who will likely never leave—
all of this living that prevents
writing or napping or reading
and toothpicks my eyes
so I don't miss any poetry.

Dead Crow Blues

The telephone wires read
like sheet music graphs.
The crows nest
like a quarter note
on the electric line.

Complimentary Seats

for Bob Pajich

We had tickets for Gillian Welch and Dave Rawlings.
Friday night at Heinz Hall. Downtown Pittsburgh.
That's Dahn Tahn, if you're from here. Our kids
back home with grandma. It was a miracle to see
friends unexpectedly seated in the row behind us.

We all waited in line for ten-dollar bourbon
in plastic cups with stirring straws and Kris
said he was working with a poet, publishing
his book The Trolleyman, and how it was
fantastic, how Pittsburgh is bursting with poets.

Scott double-fisted his beer and ten-dollar cup
behind us during the show, and Gillian Welch
apologized most of their songs were "downers"
but I was happy drinking with friends, our kids
somewhere else. Gillian even played her thighs

as percussion for a number. There was a hush
between songs and from our second-level seats
Scott yelled "You're good" loud enough
for Gillian to hear. She offered a thank you
with a bit of a curtsy, in our general direction.

PART TWO

Hunter Thompson Life Advice

They say
if you love
what you do
you never work
a day
in your life

What they don't say
is if you hate
what you do
like most of us
do, you grind
it out until death

Buy the ticket
learn to enjoy
losing

Beers With Poets, After The Reading

The night of the reading
I had $5 in my bank account
but I sold a couple books
from a cardboard box
I carried to all the readings.

Some of the poets
wanted beers afterward
and the way I saw it
I showed up with $5
and left with $45, so even

if I bought three beers
everything in my wallet
was straight profit. Usually
I declined beers. My wife,
my kids hadn't seen me yet

today, but the laughter and stories
bounced off the bottles and bubbled
out and dehydrated me into drinking
myself back down to $5. I stood
to go but the poets were still talking

about concerts and drugs and those
are some of my favorite topics so when
there was a moment, my moment, I said,
"I'm still ashamed to say I snorted coke
off the toilet paper dispenser at the casino."

A funny little antidote, I felt. But
the table went silent, not even
a courtesy laugh. Although one poet
told me she could put me in touch
with someone I could talk to, no judgement.

"Sorry," I said, assuming apology was necessary
and waved with an apathetic pageantry and walked
backward out the door and didn't feel safe
until I got to my car and turned on the music
and prepared for the drive home, drunk as I was.

Social Distortion Comes To Cheswick

We were drinking in the parking lot
of Ches Arena, a roller skating rink
turned concert venue, pre-gaming
for Social D. I bought Coors Light
from the beer shop in the nearby plaza
because my girlfriend won't drink
with me unless it's the Silver Bullet.
Werewolf killers, she calls them.

The leather jackets and chain wallets,
the pompadours and skeleton shirts
were too much for the lone police officer
who drifted through each row of the lot,
harassing concertgoers, chugging and huffing
and sniffing and smoking out of their trunks
on a Tuesday night in Cheswick, PA.

The only harassment I encountered
was from our fellow tailgaters: a woman
I worked with and her boyfriend named
Nemo, and three of their buddies passing
Jim Beam between cans of Pabst.
They said, "What do Coors Light
and Sex on the Beach have in common?
They're both fucking near water."

Nemo slurred and wobbled and when
he wasn't slugging the Beam, he was
making out with my coworker, hands
pinching, tongue slopping around her lips.
When the bottle made it back to Nemo,
he drank and handed it to his girlfriend,
who I knew better in a lanyard and a nametag.
Then Nemo started working up mucus in his throat,
stretching his neck like a reptile swallows live food whole.

He held the Jim Beam, mid-pass, an offer
to me as he spit on the ground. Except it wasn't
regular saliva-mucus spit, but more of a squirt
of vomit, a mini-puke passed off as spit.
My girlfriend and I examined the gob
of barf and instead of taking the bottle,
I clinked the neck with my werewolf killer
and said, "Cheers." Nemo seemed offended
but was coughing up something new by then.

Before he spit, he pulled my coworker close
and kissed her, open mouthed, then spewed
another Pollock-esque splotch into the lot,
so the next time the cop cruiser passed,
the tire rolled right through it, leaving
a treaded mess of bile and rock and roll
and maybe even love.

Race Relations, The Tilted Kilt, Pittsburgh, circa 2017

Tamal will not come to my home
to watch basketball this weekend.

"Not this weekend, not
next weekend. Not ever."

Tamal explains, "I'm from Philly, man.
I know about these Pittsburgh suburbs.

They'll have me strung up
in the backyard within an hour."

Tamal and I laugh. We work next
to each other at Walmart all week.

He runs the frozen and meats.
I run the bakery and produce.

We're beside each other again now
but this time on spinning barstools.

Our bartender's done up like a school girl,
our reason for landing at The Titled Kilt.

"This is beat," Tamal says and it is empty
and the waitress looks like a junkie. Nothing

here is sexy and Tamal still won't come
to my house for the Lakers and the Celtics.

"I bet there's a lot of American
flags on your street," Tamal says.

I think of porch swings shaded by flags.
Flags flapping from houses, staked in yards.

"Lots of patriots," I say and think of the kid
with a Confederate flag on the back of his quad.

I tell Tamal about the people across the street,
their grandkids. I say, "They're mixed."

"I know about that," Tamal says.
"Remember, my daughter's biracial."

I think about the word biracial, how
I said mixed. How I hope Tamal knows

I want to use the right words, but
they're just words and I really think

he could come to my house, out
in the cut, to watch some basketball.

"You gotta watch those white people
with black grandkids," Tamal says.

"Love their grandkids, not the black
man who knocked up their daughter."

With Apologies To Dave Newman

I meant no harm
by describing
your driving
bank shot layup
that gave me a P
on my driveway hoop
during a birthday party
game of PIG
as barreling

Joe

Joe stayed on dope
after his bum knee
football injury doctors
healed with a bucket of pills.

Joe went to rehab.
Joe lived with his sister
after rehab.

Joe stole rolled pennies
stashed in coffee cans
in his sister's attic
to buy a speedball.

Joe wasn't allowed
to stay with his mother
and his sister kicked him
out after the pennies
so he crashed
with his brother who cooked
at The Bistro to pay
his rent and keep
his old car running.

Joe slept on the couch
because his brother
only had two rooms.
No attic. No pennies.

Joe didn't show
for the interview washing
dishes at the Bistro.

Joe stayed home, watched
TV and ran with his friends
and told his brother he was
scared and wept in his arms.

Joe said when you
don't want to be
what you are, that's
the worst thing to be.

Joe's other sisters knew
about the drugs
about sneaking in attics
about the penny stealing
and shunned him while
his brother hugged him,
told him he loved him.

Joe told his brother he was
sorry and called a Christian
outreach group that bussed
him to a rehab clinic in Florida.

Joe didn't touch dope
for 15 months, helped
the new arrivals cope
was even named
a Junior Counsellor
by the staff at the clinic.

Joe had permanent
damage to his heart
and most of his organs.

Joe was 26 for his first
heart attack. He relapsed
only once, and that once
was all it took.
Joe had a mother
and a brother and
five sisters and
they all cried together
over a white Styrofoam box
that held all that was left of Joe.

Even Baseball Players Vote

Even baseball players vote.
They do more
than go down hacking
at a two-strike splitfinger
while we all watch
and complain
how they don't play
the game the right way
anymore.

Race Relations, Cleveland, Ohio, circa 2019

NBA games are expensive. Even
third tier, behind the backboard seats.

But Cleveland's a quick trip from Pittsburgh
where there is no NBA team. Not anymore.

My grandfather said Pittsburgh cheers
for contact sports, like hockey and football.

And baseball, he said, is America's pastime.
You have to have baseball. Pittsburgh, really

all of Western Pennsylvania, just never
took to basketball. Too soft of a sport.

Maybe. But he could
have just said racism.

My brother and I weren't born
here in Western Pennsylvania.

I claim Pittsburgh, but an Air Force Base
in North Dakota is where I was born.

My brother, in Guam. We both
want an NBA team in Pittsburgh.

The Cavaliers were terrible that year.
Lebron was long gone and Cleveland

is a quick trip from Pittsburgh. Cheap
tickets for a game played mid-week.

They call Cleveland The Land. But here
in Pittsburgh, it's The Mistake by the Lake.

My brother and I explored before tipoff.
Ate at the Hard Rock and saw the crowd

dressed like a Hot Topic commercial
for the evening's Cradle of Filth show.

We found an empty memorabilia store,
stuff for guys to display on their mantle

the loud owner explained. Said his name
was Johnny Cleveland and he didn't stop

talking for the next hour. "Everybody knows
me in this fucking town. Go ask them all."

When he heard we were from Pittsburgh
he said, "I'll try not to hold it against you."

Johnny Cleveland smelled like booze
as he talked hoops and he talked

football, how the Browns are on the rise.
He said, "Fucking Steelers better watch out."

He said he was third string quarterback,
the backup to Jim Kelly's backup.

"University of Miami," he said.
"The mother fucking U."

He showed us a blurred photo
in a wooden frame, Jim Kelly

then his backup and there, shaggy haired
and much younger: Johnny Cleveland.

"You were a quarterback there," he said,
"you could have any girl you wanted."

43

Only if Jim Kelly and his backup
didn't want them first, I joked.

Johnny Cleveland snorted, said,
"Shut the fuck up, Pittsburgh."

He said, "You know how I describe myself
back then? Young, dumb and full of cum."

Johnny laughed like he wanted us
to laugh, an affirmation of his poetry.

"All kinds of girls in Florida," he said.
"But I didn't get with any of the blacks,"

he said. "Tyra Banks or something like that?
Sure. But I just call it all monkey pussy."

Johnny Cleveland did that laugh along laugh
but the game was soon and we had to leave.

The Celtics steamrolled the Cavs
that night. Hayward scored 40 points.

Driving home, we talked out
our meeting with Johnny Cleveland

"You heard that racist stuff ?" I said.
"You mean MP?" my brother said.

"Yeah," I said. "MP."
"Fucking Cleveland."

Cleveland's just a quick trip from Pittsburgh
where we don't even have an NBA team.

Poetry Reading To Benefit Planned Parenthood

A nervous person naturally, I am
overwhelmed and edgy reading
at these events. My poems shake

up there, my throat strangled, like I drank
an ashtray. But I treat readings, especially
when the cover goes to Planned Parenthood,

like they're more important than anything
at that moment. Planned Parenthood's important
to my wife and me and people like us in need

of guidance and understanding and services
and, after having a son when we were so young,
birth control, so it wouldn't happen again.

At least with readings, where my voice
doesn't project so well and the lights
shine my forehead sweat, sometimes

I'm more drunk than I should be
and others, my poems leave them
spellbound like I'd done a magic trick.

This Planned Parenthood one, a reading
my son didn't want me to do, a reading
in a bar when I have to work in the morning,

this reading was a good one, at least
I heard people say that when I sat
and breathed and slugged a beer.

And that was sweet to hear, but I also know
writers can be a self-congratulatory bunch.
One guy even shoulder- tapped me and said,

"Good job" and I said, "Thanks,"
like I always do. This guy didn't
actually see me read, but heard

from his friends it was a good time.
"Sorry," he said, "I don't listen
to cis white males read poetry."

And I'm sure there was something
more to say there, but instead I
just said, "Thanks," like I always do.

PART THREE

Clocked In, Hanging In The Backroom

There were four
of them and one
of me circled around
the burning blunt
Monroe rolled
and the Black Velvet
Lance had cracked.

The blunt and the bottle,
the weed and the whisky
passed around like hands
of a useless clock
minute and hour
in different directions.

The Puerto Rican guy who
was maybe five foot three
who liked to act Cuban
who worked with Lance
at the cell phone kiosk
kept doing Scarface
lines like "Who do I
trust? Me," exaggerated
and hilarious to Monroe

who worked at the bank
and his friend I didn't
know but still didn't
mind drinking and smoking
with in the backroom while
Rob ran the store.
Rob always wanted hours
to pay his gram for living
in the apartment above her
to keep his Neon street legal.

Rob only smoked
when he was drinking.
Rob was the genius
behind Sailor Jerry Sundays
since we were scheduled
together every single Sunday.

I smoked and drank
and didn't think about
my mall job
my piss ant pay
my medical bills I didn't
even open, just ripped
in half and trashed,
or even my boss who'd
have fired me at the smell
of smoke in the boozy air.

And not thinking
about any of that
was kind of the point.

But before I knew the words
to say just how that felt
the whiskey appeared
on my right and the blunt
from my left like a stoner eclipse
and silence
from everyone at this meeting
of our vices, and I can honestly say
there was pressure in that
moment, so pressed
for wisdom I hit the blunt
hard and didn't exhale
but chugged Velvet instead
then let loose my smoke
in a fireball belch.

And Lance's boy
the Tony Montana guy
said, "Every day
above ground is a good day,"
and it stung like a Baptist sermon
as I crossed my arms
and passed the drugs.

Circus At The Mall

I.

The carnival popped up
In the empty JC Penney
parking lot. The Ferris wheel
was erected Wednesday
and the Wurlitzer tune
hummed through the mall
when I left work Thursday night.

II.

Friday night, two women
(one and a half, really)
showed up at my shop.
At three feet tall, one
wore a robust playoff beard
and the other was all muscles
and Naugahyde skin, eyebrows
in a permanent arch making her
look like Satan in pink spandex.

III.

Planted at my register
I saw them make a round
through the novelty store,
pretty sure I saw
the small one slip
an Insane Clown Posse ashtray down
the front of her baby doll blouse.

IV.

The body builder pinned me
to my spot with her evil eye
and lifted the little beaded lady

onto the counter and said "Hey."
She leaned into what would be
a cleavage shot for me but
her boobs, two flexed muscles
left me confused and intimidated.

V.

The circus had seemed a romantic escape
in my mind. Like freight train hopping or
riverboat card games. If they had asked me
that day to dig myself out of the cemetery
of the Galleria mall, and travel with them
in the circus, I'm not sure I could say no.

VI.

"Hey," she said again, her voice
a tractor crunching up a gravel driveway.
"Is there anything to do in this shithole?"
I shook my head, eyed the little one
for a lump the size of a stolen ashtray.
The strong lady grabbed my wrist.
I almost wept but didn't want them
to see me cry, so I stuffed it deep
into my guts and almost brought it
back up when she squeezed and asked,
"What about you, you got a girl?"

VII.

"I got two," I lied because
a hard purple vein wrapped
around her bicep. The truth
was I hadn't had a girl
in two years, except now,
this girl twisting my wrist
and winking after she said,
"Yeah, but are you happy?"

Ask Your Undertaker

Death comes
in threes, she says.

But it just seems
like you know

two other people

out of all the people
in your world

(including celebrities
and some woman

you used to work with
who died).

The living, me
and you
and the rest of the planet,

we invent

fairy tales.
We make euphemisms, religions
attempt to domesticate death.

Some of us
still hold our breath past a graveyard.

Death comes in tens, in hundreds. Some
days in thousands. Millions. Ask your undertaker
if he's only embalmed three bodies this week.

The Time I Snorted Cocaine Off A Toilet Paper Dispenser At The Rivers Casino

Each Christmas season, the Allegheny County
funeral directors fund a fancy dinner party
and even invite us, the obituary writers.

We call it the Mortician's Ball and dress up,
me in my lone jacket patched at the elbows
like a half drunk community college adjunct.

The Obituary Department was only five
underpaid writers and one of us had done this
for 25 years and declined tonight's invite.

In a casino conference room crammed with dining
tables, the four obituary writers sat with two
funeral directors and their well-dressed wives.

Both women somehow uniquely resemble
Cruella de Vil. I turned my two drink tickets
into four when the religious obit writer said

she couldn't drink. She was driving. I didn't
think about driving. I took the tickets. Not
the card for free slots after dinner. In line

for drinks as soon as they started serving,
I waited with Colin – my fellow obit writer
—and somebody yelled, "Hey!" as we finally

fell first in line. Funeral director
Mack Harrington, already red-faced,
bought our drinks, clapped our shoulders.

Mack said, "Have fun tonight, boys."
Mack said, "Never know when I'll see you next."
I asked Colin, "Why's he always say shit like that?"

55

Slot machines confuse me. So much
pageantry in pulling a lever and losing.
I wouldn't even know if I won.

Colin gave his free plays away. We watched
a blackjack table empty out and saw it was
the only one with a five dollar buy-in.

It seemed obscene to hold my
50 dollars, in chips, between
my thumb and forefinger. One

of the women from our dinner table,
Cruella Number Two, wiggled away
with her chips clacking in a steel bucket.

The only two at the table, I was up
15 bucks, drowning in beginners luck.
Colin whispered when the dealer shuffled.

Colin said, "You only count face cards."
Colin said, "If they deal you a pair, split 'em."
Colin said, "You want to go to the bathroom?"

Rivers Casino doesn't provide free beer and I was out
of drink tickets, so I counted my chips in beers: I was down
to four beers so I said, "Yeah, let's go to the bathroom."

Colin said, "I have something, but it's not
the usual something" which meant not
smoking pot in the newspaper parking lot.

The casino bathroom was well-lit but not clean.
Most importantly, it was empty. Colin stepped out
from a stall and handed me one rolled dollar.

A choppy white line waited on top
of the toilet paper dispenser and before
I stuffed the bill up my right nostril,

before I pressed my casino chip against
my other nostril and sniffed deep and cleaned
that toilet paper dispenser, I thought:

That looks kind of dirty. What if my heart
seizes after sniffing this? What if my wife
claims my corpse on the bathroom floor?

I thought: Surely, there are enough
funeral directors here tonight
if I do suffer sudden death.

I thought about blackjack and gambling
for chips, which are money here, gambling
for death, which is money here as well.

I inhaled the line, shook my nose. My feet
made sticky noises when I stepped and a piece
of toilet paper teetered on the face of the seat.

The Accountant

Read a book of poems and it stole his breath. There was an image,
a mallard-head-handled umbrella that really struck him. The beak
yellow and flaking with age. Eyes as black and endless as an oil spill.

The Accountant saw numbers in his head. He multiplied
and divided faster than machines and he barely tried. He
was assembled that way, but The Accountant couldn't write.

His words were planks and his hands were splintered
but he couldn't exert control over the words
the way he could with percentages and spreadsheets.

The Accountant went home in tears on a Thursday evening
and his wife asked if he had been stung by a bee and if she
should grab the Epi-Pen. The Accountant searched the cupboard

where a bottle of bourbon—opened two years ago when they hosted
Christmas dinner, then immediately re-sealed —stayed out of sight. But
The Accountant was seeing out-of-sight things and he blamed

the poetry book and the umbrella and every duck he'd seen since. He
poured a tumbler half full while his wife cried because he skipped
dinner, but The Accountant was only hungry for the right words now.

After two hours he had finished his half-glass, and had written
exactly five words and they were not very good words. He read
the clock and knew he had twelve hours and twenty-two minutes

until he would wake for work where numbers would spin inside him
like a slot machine and the thought of not writing a great poem tonight
became a bag over his head and he wondered if maybe he had been stung

not by a bee, but by a poem, or maybe a stinging species
of mallard. He wanted anti-venom. He wanted to muzzle
the fire inside his mind. He read his five words aloud:

"I really don't like bourbon." His daughter staggered
from the hallway, in pajamas he noticed, perhaps,
for the first time, decorated with ducks floating downstream.

Ducks with jade heads. Mallards. And his daughter
said, "Daddy, I thought I heard you saying crazy things -"
and The Accountant looked at his five words, felt

a small satisfaction he could not calculate.
He dropped his pen in the bourbon, kissed
his daughter's head and waltzed her back to sleep.

PART FOUR

Box Store Urine Cup

I.

This was all before. Before I left office work and willingly jumped back into retail, into the life I now have, working at Walmart. I'll circle back to the beginning after the break.

The first day was a blur.

The second day, I broke two bones in my foot hauling a glacier of Aquafina and Gatorade from a delivery truck. I had never touched a pallet jack in my life. I wanted to make a good impression. The delivery driver who witnessed the wheels of the pallet jack roll onto my foot, smirked beneath his white beard and trucker cap. I tried not to scream. He watched me push the shrink-wrapped stack of beverages with both hands and yank myself free. He came at me clipboard first, in need of a signature while I grimaced and massaged my ankle.

The delivery driver said, "Hope you got some steel toes in there."

I contemplated my $40 Vans.

"No," I said. "I don't."

It felt like my toes were trying to eat my foot.

They sent me to the Med-Express, the one they always use, and the doctor there needed one glance at my damaged foot, swollen and scraped bloody, purple up to my ankle. My pinkie toenail black and half missing.

The doctor looked, then looked away then said, "Oh yeah. That's broken."

I sat there for an hour, soaked my foot in a pan before the x-rays, worried the whole time if I'd make it back to my new job at Walmart tomorrow.

II.

It has been 13 days since I've been high.

I chug a urine dilution drink that tastes like Nyquil and Hawaiian Punch an hour before walking into Med-Express for my piss test and I still taste it when I burp. Back at home, I peed into red Solo cups and passed my Amazon-ordered THC test three times, but I still wretch my hands when I speak to the unsmiling, scrub-wearing woman at triage.

Sheryl—at least that's on her bronze bar of a nametag—is an MA, I assume. She is close to my age, 39, maybe a little younger. She smiles when she says, "You're here for a drug test?"

I'm not totally convinced it's a bad idea to crack a small, humorous comment until I hear myself say, "I've been drinking all day, so I don't get stage fright."

Sheryl assumes I mean beer or bourbon, that I'm making an alcoholism joke. Really, I've chugged two $20 bottles of this dilution drink to cover up my pot habit.

Sheryl smiles sympathetically and says, "Oh. Okay."

Sheryl is a dark-rooted, unnatural blond and stocky. She's thick-legged and buoyant and I follow her to a small gray desk. I do as I'm told and lay my yellow and black Pirates cap on the counter. I set the contents of my pockets—keys, wallet, cell phone—inside the hat, like placing candy in a bowl. I wonder what Sheryl looks like stoned, if she gets high. I'm sure her job here, working with the public, is filled with stress.

Except for the past 13 days, I regularly used pot as a post-work reward. A treat for slogging through the everyday bullshit of a job I hated, and a reason to button my shirt and do it all again the next day.

Sheryl says, "First door on the right," and points down a door-lined hallway, then to a blue line ringing the plastic cup she holds between her thumb and finger. "Try to void up to the line. A little more is better than a little less."

I grin. "Is that what I'm doing? Voiding?"

For the first time, Sheryl smiles. She says, "Job terminology."

"I hear you," I say. "Every job has its own language. That's what this is all about. I'm trying to get a job at Walmart. There's no other reason to test me, you know."

Sometimes, when I'm nervous or awkward—as in most of the time—I can't shut the fuck up. Instead I fill the space between me and any stranger with words and stack them together like a mason until there's a wall to hide behind.

"Make sure you do not flush or wash your hands until this cup is back in my possession," Sheryl says and gives me the cup.

I say, "Thanks," and flick the light switch and the heavy bathroom door clicks closed behind me. I fill myself with the sterile bleached scent of the room. The constant buzz of the overhead light is the only sound in the holding cell-sized restroom until I start to piss. First in the toilet, then, mid-stream, I slide over to the cup and fill it. I void.

I read online you don't want to start or end peeing in the cup. That's where the drugs hide. You want them to test the middle of the piss. I don't know if that's true or not, but at this point I'm willing to try anything.

III.

My intermediary job, the one between writing obituaries and working at Walmart, was for an accounting and payroll firm. It was an unexpected job offer following the death of the old billionaire, Richard Scaife, Pittsburgh philanthropist and newspaper owner.

I have too many debts and bills to not have a job. I have two sons who rely on my job for food and clothes and everything else children need in life. I need a car, my wife needs a car. Mostly to go back and forth to work. We are work bots and always low on money.

The paper I worked at offered buyouts. The paper laid off twice a year. I didn't get a raise the last two. I was never offered a buyout, as there was a bit more job security in obituaries than the classifieds and accounting and HR. When the relative of a friend offered me the job at his five-person accounting firm on Pittsburgh's North Side, I shook his hand and signed the contract.

I put in a one-week notice at the paper. My boss, a salt-and-pepper, spikey-haired man with a thin-mustached goatee he spent too much time sculpting, was professional, diplomatic, but I knew. He was glad to see me go. We had clashed about the main objective of the Obituary Department a couple times before. I felt we not only respectfully memorialized the Western Pennsylvanians who lived, worked and died in this area with flawless accuracy and authenticity, but to do so according the grammatical protocols of the Associated Press.

My boss said I was there to make money for the paper.

"How much more are they paying you?" he asked from behind his paper-cluttered desk.

"A dollar more an hour," I said. The resignation letter I typed and signed flapped in his hand as he spoke.

"I certainly can't knock a man for doing what's best for him, but," he looked down at the resignation letter, then up at me. He sucked some air before he spoke. "I wish I had more time to find your replacement. You've only given me one week."

I stood, scooted my chair with the backs of my knees. I said, "I did," and stepped to the closed office door. I cradled and door handle, but didn't turn.

I glared back to my boss rocking in his chair, my two-sentence resignation in his hand. Inside his goatee, I saw him smirk. A bullseye for my $40 vans.

"I gave you the last seven years," I said and made sure to slam the door behind me.

IV.

A year into my new job, the intermediary payroll office job, I began looking for a new one. I worked from home four days a week and hated it. Working from the couch, daytime television droning in the background, processing an endless amount of Medicaid billing claims on behalf of a home healthcare provider, made me miserable. It was work a robot should do. There was no writing, no thinking, no creativity—a vital need in keeping my death-obsessed mood in check. I was depressed and taking pills for that and smoking dope for the pills and drinking at night to forget about the days.

"Honestly," I told my wife. "The best thing I can do for this family is leave you with a nice life insurance policy."

Even though I commuted one day a week, the drive to

66

the North Side was brutal. The morning drive on the Parkway East, through the Squirrel Hill Tunnels, took at least an hour, usually more. The ride home was worse. Pittsburgh traffic turned an eight-hour day into an 11-hour excursion. The days from home weren't any better. The solitude fed into the feelings eating away inside me, like a black hole in my guts. I needed interaction with people I wasn't related to. My wife and kids were great, but I thrived in environments where I exchanged ideas and conservations with others, jobs where I knew I was helping someone. Not this. Not fixing dates and amounts and watching a bouncing circle on a computer screen to see if a claim was accepted or not.

When the Department of Education called to say they were garnishing my wages, 15 percent of my take home pay, for student loans I'd taken out for a degree that kept me employed at jobs that barely paid the bills, I knew we were fucked.

"That's it," I said. "We're fucked. Our lives are fucked."

"What about Walmart?" My wife said. "I heard they pay well."

"I guess," I said. "It seems like half the country already works there."

"What about your resume?" she said. "Did you send it?"

"Yeah," I said. "But you know. It is Walmart. Would I really want to work there?"

PART FIVE

My Grandmother, The Judas

After the meal, my grandfather
and dad and uncles flopped
on armchairs and loveseats
and cheered for the Steelers.

The kids, we ran outside, rolled
down the fresh-cut hill, jumped
off the massive yellow rock
in the front yard and tackled
each other until somebody got hurt.

The women stayed at the table
played Scrabble and told stories
and cackled and cried until
my grandfather turned up
the game in silent rebuttal.

My mom told her mom,
how Father John said
after Communion—
after my grandmother slipped
out to start this Sunday supper—
that Judas was always
the first to leave church.

Porch swing cigarette in hand,
my grandmother said, "The same
Father John who drove
drunk and now blesses
grape juice instead of wine?"

The Last Diary Entry of Judas Iscariot

Before you judge me,
I was a fan of the guy.

He was kind
and had a way of telling
stories that stuck with you,
even though he was nearly a gypsy.
I mean, Jesus, he was a good guy.

When I was drunk and crazy
with lust, Jesus found me. He
breathed empathy and cared
about all us poor people. Jesus
was poor too, really into carpentry.
I still have the fish he carved from
an oak tree and gave me for my birthday.

Then Jesus got all weird
about our wives and
about drinking his blood
and eating his body.

Even Thomas, who wouldn't
believe anything unless you
put it right under his nose swore
Jesus was some drunken savant.

It wasn't a paying gig,
following him around.
I have debts.
My family and friends
die in the streets,
slaughtered for beliefs.

I didn't feel too terrible
talking to the Romans
with their sun-dried muscles
and short shorts and leather
straps across their chests.
Their leaders were a class
above our own, real royalty,
not afraid of the throne.

They said I was admiral,
a testament to my people,
promised me a key role
in the gentrification
of our Sand Belt community.

But then, in the garden,
when Jesus kissed my cheek,
forgave me like he knew
what was happening – that
was my lowest point, Christ,
he even healed the guard's ear
after Pete chopped it off.

I got the rope from James.
He used to bind wood together,
called them Jimmy's Rafts.
Found a sturdy branch
on a proud pecan tree
and tossed my 30 coins
into the sky
tossed myself
into the sky.
They say you could hear
the crack
over in Jerusalem.

But please, don't hate
me for selling Jesus out.
If I didn't someone else
surely would have talked.

Like I said, Jesus was
a fortune teller. The dark
distracted look under his
dusty long hair. He could
read your soul with a glance.

Plus, I got in on that
whole absolution of sin.

I am forgiven and free now.

My Grandfather, From Abruzzo

His parents came off
the boat.

He didn't listen
when they told him to stay away
from those women from Sicily.

"Called them Fast Marys,"
he said and my grandmother
as loud and Sicilian as they come
laughed and I didn't
really understand but
was old enough to pretend I did.

I asked for more buttered bread
and my grandfather
swiped his knife along the towel
slung over his shoulder and sliced
a hunk

from the soft loaf, cradled
the bread like a robin's egg
and spread the butter quick
and thin, as the crust flaked,
sprinkled onto the tabletop.

Crack Dance

It was Officer Scotty Haymaker's move.
An end zone dance mixed with a bit
of Funky Chicken whenever he found
crack—or meth or pills—really any type

of drugs. And in Johnstown,
there's a lot of people
taking drugs
selling drugs
cooking drugs
prescribing drugs.

Drugs are the new flood
around here. Doctors are broken
spillways, sign papers in waves,
watch people just wash away.

All the cops touched you up
in the elevator. No cameras there.

My dad, the cop, said sometimes
it gets stuck. The elevator.
He said, "They come in talking
shit. By the second floor, they
don't have much to say."

There's a traffic light
in Kernville where
you don't even have
to stop if it's red.

Here's where Officer Scotty Haymaker
chased a kid down. This kid, he stuffed
his mouth as he ran, like popcorn bits.

Here's where Officer Scotty Haymaker
bounced the kid's head off the cement
until he spit the drugs and his teeth into the street.

Here's where Officer Scotty Haymaker
held a crack rock up to the flashlight, a jewel
mined from the depths of our own cemeteries.

And here's where Officer Haymaker
did his Crack Dance,
all elbows and kneecaps, above
the handcuffed kid facedown
beat up and bleeding on the ground.

My dad smiled, shook his head,
said, "Scotty's crazy."

I said, "Was he okay?"
meaning the kid with the busted teeth.

"That guy?"
my dad said.
"Fuck that guy."

The Night Regis Got Rolled

Oh sure, I knew the guy.
Ten years on midnight shift,
you get acquainted
with the late-night crowd.

He stalked around
the gas pumps, talking
himself into it, his hands
stuffed into his Starter jacket.

I already counted the cigarettes
and swept the candy and chip
aisles. Made sure I had enough
pennies to get through the bar rush.
I was just about to fill the wash bucket
and wipe the prints off the cooler doors.

He said, "Well, you know me,
so give me the money."

I said, "You need to show me
a weapon first, don't you?"

He had this busted piece of pipe,
bashed the air between us
like he'd crack my head.

I said, "Here you go," and gave him
the forty bucks in the register, all
ones and fives. Just made a drop
ten minutes earlier. Then he wanted
the silver too, so I tied off a plastic bag.

The worst part happened
when Corporate called
the next day, some kid
who sounded 12 years old,
but Christ this was noon
and I sleep until 2:30.

He wanted assurance
I wouldn't sue
and told me I could take off
the next two days. Paid.

I said, "No.
It'd just mess up
my sleep schedule."

Race Relations, Texaco Gas Station, Johnstown, PA, circa 1996

The line runs along the milk
coolers, blocking the ATM.

The crew deep fries chicken,
reheats precooked burgers,
yelling order numbers above
the grumble of impatient patrons.

"Number 17,"
calls one of the crew,
a small, white woman
frazzled and unsmiling.

"Number 17."
Again.

Nobody speaks so she raises
the black plastic container
like a Ten Commandment
tablet above her netted hair
and shouts, "Chicken salad.
Who's got it?"

I work food service. I know
her contempt for this moment,
her urge to just push through,
knowing this will be a blur, later.

One thing I don't do
is eat salad. But, I
really wanted my
sausage
bagel
cheese

mayo
sandwich
because Nick's brother
needs a ride to buy
us a party ball to drink
out in the woods tonight.

So I raise up, look the crowd
over, trying to make eye contact
and the only one who connects
is a black guy who seems
the same age as me, hungry
just like me, so I say, "You
order a chicken salad?"

He says, "I don't eat
no chicken salad, you
racist motherfucker."

I Never Did Get That Job

Bi-Lo Grocery ripped my
application from a stack
of copies. My first chance
at a lifetime of employment.

The hair-netted cashier never smiled
but I thanked her. Made my way
across scuffed linoleum and the scent
of cardboard and elderly shoppers.

I wrote my name neatly
on the line, chose my words
like they were the epitaph
of my own tombstone.

My entire work experience
was a blank, and I was full
of confusion for what position
I was qualified to even apply.

I thought I knew work.
My grandfather swept
the streets. My grandmother
sewed mattresses in a factory.

Both first generation.
Both my parents gone
most days, working. Me
watching the kids at home.

Stalker.
That's what I wrote
on the line for the job
I desired at their store.

Slayer In A Dress Shirt

We celebrated at the Claddagh, off the crawl
of bars along Carson Street. Slayer in a dress shirt,
all Easter pastels, a suit jacket he bought with his
five finger discount. Slayer's nickname stuck
since high school, when he wore metal shirts
exclusively. We ate appetizers, chugged fancy beers.

Though I promised several months prior
to abstain from tequila in public, I shot mine
down and slammed the glass on the bar
and hooted with the rest of them. This was not
the first promise I'd broken with myself.
I'd chugged three five-hour energy shots
on Wednesday before my double-shift at the mall,
where my chest cramped and my sweat stained
my polo collar and I felt my heart slam inside
of me like someone dribbling a basketball.

Like most lies I tell myself, I usually drink them.

Slayer showed us the jagged sliver along the lip
of his shot glass. I ran a finger around the rim,
pricked the tip at the crack and said, "You should
show the bartender this. You could cut your lip open."

Slayer grabbed his lip with his thumb and forefinger
and tore. He tore again. Then pulled his bottom lip
from both corners, stretched the growing gash and
flagged the bartender, showed her the shot glass.
She almost laughed, but when she saw the blood
she disappeared. A manager replaced her, offered
Slayer a napkin for the blood spot on his chin.

The manager said, "Are you okay now?"
He said, "Obviously, your drinks are free

for the rest of the night." And that was it,
that's why Slayer was willing to suffer.
Free beer. Free fancy beer. Totally worth
the blood in my opinion. In fact, I'd appreciate
some beer for my own suffering. Over promises
I break. Over heart breaks. Over line breaks.

But when you work with the public, you know
the world's suffering is always greater
than your own. Some people can't even dream
about appetizers and fancy beers and tequila.

Slayer chugged two beers in 30 seconds
and came back with another and slid me
a new Shock Top and said, "Looks like
you could use a refill" and any time I was
almost empty, he brought another cold one.

He dipped his napkin in ketchup, daubed his lip
for appearances, but the manager said we were
cut off and should leave. Slayer slipped his hand
around the waist of some guy's girlfriend and spit
into two ashtrays. He pointed at the manager, slurred
"Don't piss down my back and tell me it's raining."

I've known Slayer since high school. We drank
in the woods and passed out in sleeping bags
or sometimes with nothing but the Johnstown dirt
beneath us. That's what happened to me so that's
who I am. But I've been that manager too, surviving
two more hours of madness for five hours of sleep.

Outside, Carson Street boomed a soundtrack
of traffic that glowed under the stoplights, and
the bars teemed with lines of drunks and I
thanked Slayer for the beers. He told me
we'd be even if I blocked the view as he
puked down the steps of a basement apartment.

The First Person I Fell In Love With Was on TV

It wasn't just the cleavage. I mean
I was an eight-year-old boy and she
was Elvira, Mistress of the Dark.

It had to do with colors too.
Her skin like an eggshell
that could've cracked open.
Under absurd lipstick, her face
brutally rogued around the edges.

And all that black. Black
eyeliner. Black stockings.
Black hair pouffed into
a storm cloud and falling
to her shoulders to a neckline
that tapered down to her navel.

My small finger smudged
the screen tracing it all
the way down to her belly
and below. Down to her skirt,
the high-riding slit up one side.
Thighs and calves,
were all part of it too.

My small finger smudged
the screen tracing it all
the way down. And sometimes,
when I wasn't fast enough,
a commercial would flash
and my finger stuck there
pointing at collectable presidential
coins or some other gimmick on TV.

PART SIX

TWENTY-SIX

Driving Through The Old Neighborhood

My first apartment is now
a patch of yellow grass.

I lived on the top floor
shacked up with my girl

who waitressed and paid
half the rent. We ate food

I brought home from my job
at the deli and our fridge

held beer and condiments.
We watched bad horror movies

and fell asleep or fucked
on the hand-me-down couch.

Days off, we slept until noon.
Betty lived downstairs

and complained Clydesdales
trotted up and down our steps

every time I walked them
after the dayshift at the deli.

Wouldn't have my boots off
yet and she'd bang the broom

against the ceiling, bitching
she couldn't hear her stories.

Betty sat on her porch, her cats
tied to the posts with twine ropes.

You could smell cat piss and death
reeking from her apartment. Once

she showed us her yearbook,
1931, black and white photos

pasted to stapled-together
black construction paper.

My own senior yearbook
a photo I force-smiled for

only three years ago, was binned
in the attic of my childhood home.

But now, Betty's dead
and the apartment's gone

and the homes of our old neighbors
are decayed and broken, porches

loaded with junk. There's
an opioid crisis here now.

There was always
an opioid crisis here.

A group of girls stand
in the pot-holed streets,

block my path out of here
and scowl, take their time.

I beep and see them talk
shit but the music's up

and all I hear from this town is
I love you, I love you, I love you.

ACKNOWLEDGEMENTS

Appreciation and gratitude to the editors and publishers where some of these poems first appeared.

An earlier version of "The Spider" appeared in *The Pittsburgh Post-Gazette.*

"Complimentary Seats" and "One Week Notice" and "Social Distortion Comes To Cheswick" were first published in *Nerve Cowboy* (my favorite lit mag). Thanks to Joe, Jerry, and Elissa.

Thank you to Joshua at *Sterling Clack Clack* for accepting "Box Store Urine Cup" for publication as well.

about the author

Adam Matcho is the author of the essay collection, *The Novelty Essays,* as well as two collections of poetry: *Love Songs From Flood City* and *$6 an Hour: Confessions of a Gemini Writer.*

His poems and essays have been widely published in such places as *The Pittsburgh Post-Gazette, Nerve Cowboy, Chiron Review, Tears in the Fence, Sterling Clack-Clack,* and elsewhere.

A graduate of the writing program at The University of Pittsburgh-Greensburg and a YMCA basketball coach, he works as a manager of a big-box store somewhere in America and lives in Apollo, PA with his family.